SOFIA
Gubaidulina/SONATA (1965)
TIGRAN
Mansurian/SONATA (1967)

TWO PIANO SONATAS

Anglo-Soviet Music Press, London
Sole Selling Agents:
Boosey & Hawkes, Music Publishers Ltd.
for Great Britain and British Commonwealth of Nations (except Canada)

Le Chant du Monde, Paris
pour la France, Belgique, Luxembourg et les Pays francophones de l'Afrique

Japan-Soviet Music Inc., Tokyo
for Japan

G. Ricordi & C., Milano
per l'Italia

Musikverlag Hans Sikorski, Hamburg
*für die Bundesrepublik Deutschland einschl. West-Berlin, Griechenland, Israel,
Niederlande, Portugal, Schweiz, alle skandinavischen Länder, Spanien und Türkei*

ISBN 978-0-7935-3820-1

Associated Music Publishers, Inc.

DISTRIBUTED BY

HAL•LEONARD™
CORPORATION
7777 W. BLUEMOUND RD. P.O. BOX 13819 MILWAUKEE, WI 53213

Piano Sonata

Sofia Gubaidulina (1965)

I

*) Glissando on piano pegs with bamboo stick.

AMP-7618

* Hold string with left hand.

*Strike the string in low register with the fingers.

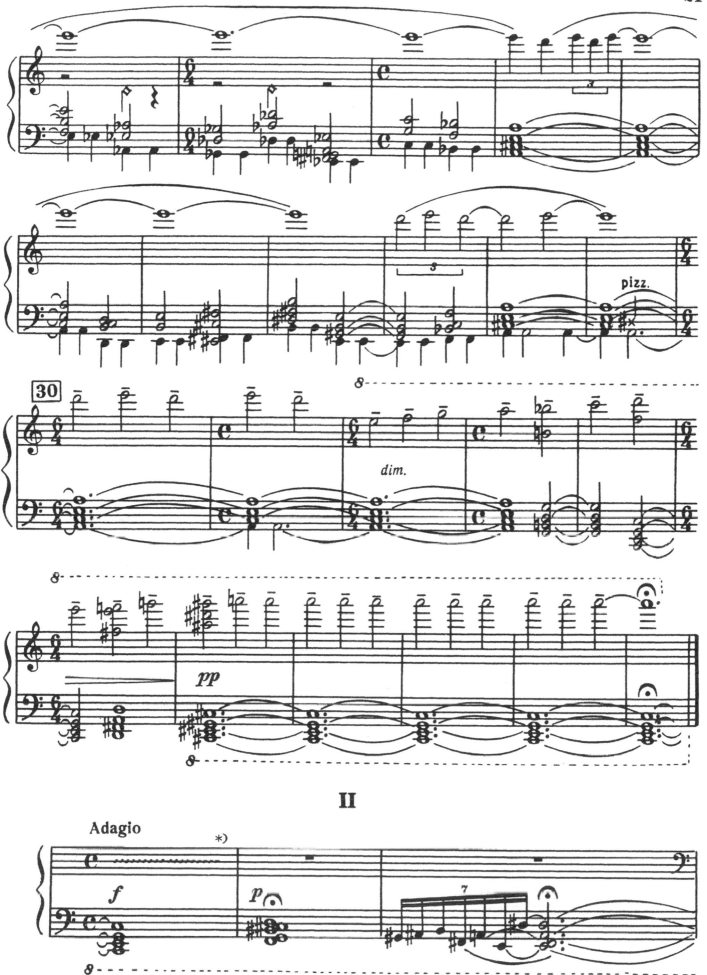

II

Adagio

*Glissando on piano pegs with bamboo stick.

22

* Strike the strings in low register with the fingers.

** Place the bamboo stick on the vibrating strings.

AMP-7618

* Glissando with fingernails on lowest strings.

** Performers may use this version of the cádenza for improvisaton on any notes.

*** Strike the strings in low register with the fingers.

AMP-7618

* Strike the strings in low register with the fingers.

AMP-7618

III

Allegretto

Dedicated to L. M. Sarian

Sonata
for Piano

I

Tigran Mansurian (1967)

Tempo colla construzione della musica

Piano

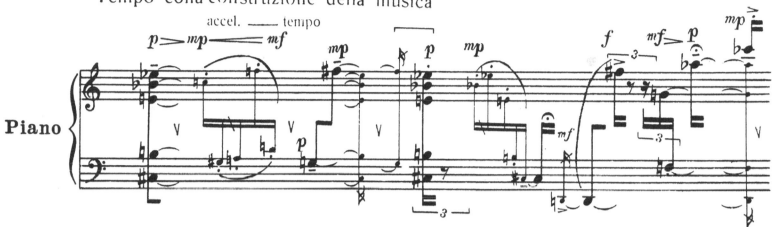

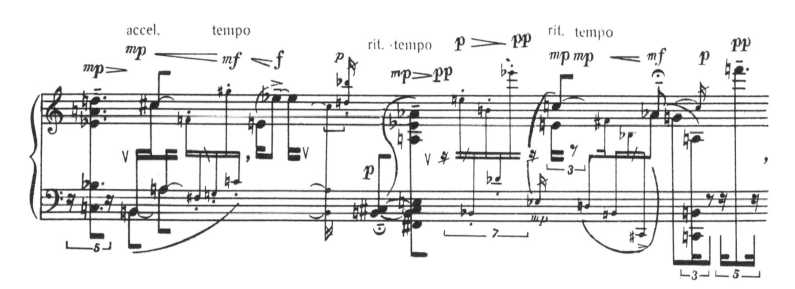

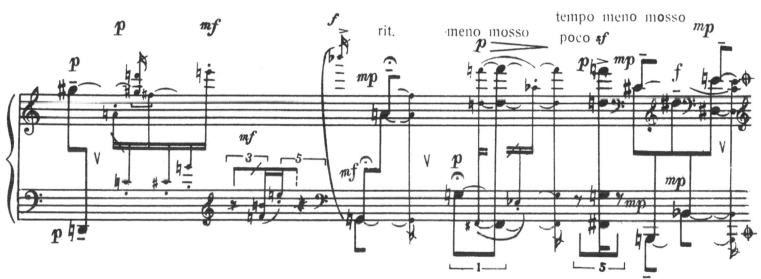

AMP-7618

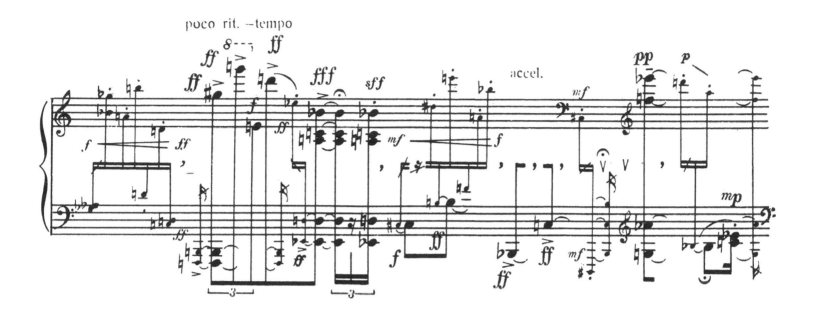

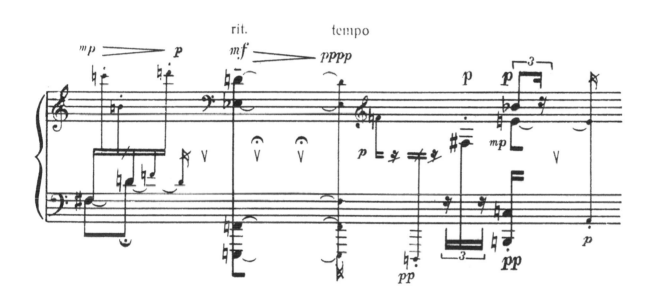

III